THREE
SEA
STONES

VASILIKI KATSAROU

THREE
SEA
STONES

SOLITUDE HILL PRESS
ANNANDALE, NEW JERSEY

First published in a limited handbound edition in 2020
by MaryAnn L. Miller at Lucia Press, Clinton, New Jersey, USA

First paperback edition in 2023 by Solitude Hill Press,
Annandale, New Jersey, USA

Cover art is from an original serigraph and pochoir by
MaryAnn L. Miller

ISBN 979-8-9855927-1-9
www.solitudehill.com

CONTENTS

DOVECOTE

in a frame above the stairs
ink sketch of a Greek soubrette
in feathered hat and fur muffler

she looks away—

so far away
her features cannot be gathered back

her expression is a dove
flown so far ahead of us

its shadow has returned to perch
here

peristerióna
     dovecote

you who flit and fly
alongside

such eyes
you never meet
but in this niche

rise

high above the white hills of the island

ELEMENTS

Light: first source
of fruit,

fruit: gifts of the tree
and the sea,

see, seek shelter in its shade

let shade scissor light
from dark

weave

we've a pattern
of these elements

and draw from them a home

dance in its shadow

Time
   whirls
through us demi-
      urgically

let the wind connect us
to the tree

let the rain connect us
to the sea

THREE SEA STONES

Kiato stone

like a bean or an unformed heart
girdled, ringed, cleft by a river of white
given in green, parched in earth

Patmos stone

Aztec puzzle,
bull's heart with stippled on
arteries of blood

Pollock of the fingertips

Paros stone

beloved button
earth-sewn, your pastel skin
is heaven's evidence

SIFNOS / BRESSON

An image in silver
of a Sifnos street
today at Swann Galleries
in Manhattan
starting bid: 3,000 dollars

There solid sheets of light
rain down on ancient
cypress

now ciphers

Beyond the sea
is another form of transparency

What art is there
to make need
of these elements

When sky is another medium
of light,

and existence, an invitation to love
within webs of blood

Once, Sifnos
had silver and gold

potters, poets,
a treasury at Delphi

hills terraced
like beehives

Then farmers, poets
and potters resolved
to sell gilded lead
as gold

all the veins of Sifnos
ran cold

Centuries passed
the sea was glass

a Venetian town stacked
on its ruins:
paleometropolis

The Chapel of Seven Martyrs
set on barren rocks
has the dimensions
of Thoreau's cabin

if Thoreau were Greek Orthodox
and a thousand years old

What need is there
to make art of these elements

Now that the stone footpaths
are empty

the child in the photo has gone

and Sifnos is a ship at sea

Yet the exhilaration of shadow
and vastness persists,

the light and odd sense of loss

lies

just around the bend

in the immensities
of "let's pretend"

THE CUTTLEFISH

The cuttlefish has no skull
and three hearts
so it must camouflage

The cuttlefish has three hearts
but no backbone
to survive it must dazzle

unveil electric skin, myriad intersecting
iridescences, an ever unspooling
film of itself—

a screen that is a mirror
that is a screen—

The cuttlefish has three hearts
but no skill

a mouth hidden inside its mouth
& teeth on its tongue

to survive you
it must dazzle, use subterfuge

leave song and self
unbidden swirl

off its
inky skin

BLACK & WHITE

in my front yard is a white horse
in my backyard is a black crow

in the front tree is a black plastic wing
torn from somewhere I don't know

in the backyard is a white plastic
chair, marking the spot
legs in the air

in a backward glance
is a white cat
weaving through legs
at every pass

the black cat crows
the black plastic blows

the white horse gets sold
the white plastic chair
lies upside down

marks the spot in the air
where the tree will grow

FLÂNEUSE

First, she suggests little icons for part titles
and mentions "the poetry of the leafless garden"
where flower becomes fruit then drops into rot
and finally she says "just think about yourself"

On the way to meet her,
the streets are paved with paper

I lease empty rooms in Paris
under the sign of Minerva

while in Mina Loy's armory
up shoot silos of red
and artificial æther

by noon the crêperie will be owned by Greeks
from Athens who note my name
without confusion

Day leads me through
when the line goes dead
rooms open up before me

in New York, in Arezzo
the fictive couple decide to separate
or celebrate another anniversary

we smiled, said goodbye
and in the crumbs left behind
on the table

a poem was lifted whole
from the day that contained it

like a pie from its plate

Where I step is muck
                    is lily

smoke that makes the light visible

part the silver drape of afternoon

                    to see

wisteria hysteria:

                    all these are
                    but
                    soul tethers

MY HOUSE IS A BOOK

My house is a book
with a sewn spine

Its pages are walls
torn all from all

Each year looses its script
lets slip its alembic of fresco
and ochre,

sperm curls wiggle
beneath the painted plaster

stare back at me
from some Minoan dream

Tear into a corner here
and it is 1843

nothing ruined yet
and no one I know

No bridal chamber
stripped bare

All still legible, before drywall
still life partitioned
into rooms, into moods

Back when
silence and detritus
reigned coincident

TERRARIUM

once
I thought
I saw
my soul in miniature

a bonsai
magnified inside
a glass terrarium

the flowering tree
and the One
wielding the ax

as the tree grows
so
it hones the ax

PITH

they line the transits like ordnance
guide the cow cars
keep me moving in straight lines
no matter parallel or perpendicular

peek and roll through rusting leaf piles
inedible unbounceable fodder
all rind and pith

but for the countless bitter seeds
of paleohorses

NOSTALGIA OF THE APPLE TREE

apple trees are rooted, gnarled
apple trees belong
apple trees are *dopia,* local

immigrants are not apple trees
immigrants are uprooted
apple trees are not olive trees

poets are uprooted
olive trees are millennia old

uprooted poets who strive
toward the sun

are floating and subject
to wind gusts

nostalgia of the apple tree
and the olive grove

of the tender loam of home

CYCLADIA

1.
Slim round pastel
Cycladic stones

I turn over
in my palm

as the sun darkens
me to the shade
of pale wood

2.
I found a knucklebone
sea pebble chiseled by time
into die

I found a cuttlefish bone
ovoid obole
stone almost
balsa wood

Coins of no realm
cast ashore

scoured of their stamps
eyed and palmed

awaiting traces
of us

3.
Sifnos means empty
le gouffre, quoi
Each terrassed hill—
pyramidal—
an inverse vessel

to carry us
from Iron Age to plastics

and this graffitied amphora
a cipher of modernity

4.
Cuttlefish bone, sea stone:
history

is leaving our marks
before the obole arrives

obsolete
at its destination

THE LETTERS

are what remains
what the son couldn't toss
elegant convoluted cursive
strokes in a second language

tabled scraps of
far-flung lives, entangled
faith, education abroad

record of a botched surgery,
a car accident, but also piano recitals,
late birthday telegrams: *My son, may you live
as long, as tall as these hills*

all shoved in a drawer,
vagaries and vagrancy
he won't consider too closely now

this full moon August
when another family of strangers
occupies the family house

listens to the morning and the noontime bells
plots a happy return
to the summer island

PRIMARY

The sun parted the painted clouds

rent a sun-sized hole
in my dingy tableau

    a reality-hole

wiped clear years of hesitation
and tobacco smudge

So the dancers with red aprons,
stymied by music-less decades

gazed at the real sun in their artificial world
and lifted their skirts

to take one
tarantella step
forward

VERGE

Blue flames out on a ground of gold
and the dismantled virgin
cloaks her own decoction

Red fruit, and likely, black leaf rot
is the fraught ground of most
wisdom

All flaws bloom lately
on the demented cheek
of the virgin
crowned now with blue bachelor buttons

Don't fret
that we sought flaws, not flowers
dots, not bowers nor dowry

Search the underbrush
for the one undying branch
that sprouts its omega leaves

NEW NAXOS

Still air circling
above the arid hills of Naxos
spiked with agave and half-toppled
miniature cedars
tilting at

      witnessing
      the end
      or perhaps this is how
      the earth starts over

ACKNOWLEDGEMENTS

La Vague Journal: "Black & White" and "The Cuttlefish"

Wild River Review: "Sifnos / Bresson"

Regime Journal (AUSTRALIA): "Cycladia"

Noon: Journal of the Short Poem (JAPAN): "Where I step is muck, is lily"

U.S. 1 Worksheets: "Nostalgia of the Apple Tree," "Flâneuse" and "Dovecote"

Agave Magazine: "My House Is a Book"

Climate of Opinion: Sigmund Freud in Poetry: "Terrarium"

Contemporary American Voices and *Meta-Land: Poets of the Palisades II:* "Primary" and "Elements"

Tiferet: Writing and the Creative Spirit: "The Letters"

Nature and Death, pamphlet by Corbel Stone Press (U.K.): "New Naxos"

Otoliths (AUSTRALIA): "Pith"

"Verge" was written for *Transactions*, an art+poetry exhibition, Spinning Plate Gallery, Pittsburgh